U0435470

WESTERN CHINA SCIENCE AND TECHNOLOGY INNOVATION HARBOUR

中国西部科技创新港

主　编　李晓鸣　程洪莉
副主编　董　琪　朱建欣　刘鸿翔

图书在版编目（CIP）数据

港之风帆/李晓鸣，程洪莉主编．—西安：
西安交通大学出版社，2020.8（2021.4重印）
ISBN 978-7-5693-1754-1

Ⅰ.①港… Ⅱ.①李… ②程… Ⅲ.①地方高校—产学研一体化—建设—概况—西安 Ⅳ.①G649.2

中国版本图书馆CIP数据核字（2020）第095129号

书　　名	港之风帆
主　　编	李晓鸣　程洪莉
副 主 编	董　琪　朱建欣　刘鸿翔
责任编辑	王斌会　蔡乐芊
责任校对	侯君英
出版发行	西安交通大学出版社
	（西安市兴庆南路1号　邮政编码710048）
网　　址	http://www.xjtupress.com
电　　话	（029）82668357　82667874（发行中心）
	（029）82668315（总编办）
传　　真	（029）82668280
印　　刷	西安五星印刷有限公司
开　　本	787mm×1092mm　1/12　印　张 10.5　字　数 140千字
版次印次	2020年8月第1版　2021年4月第3次印刷
书　　号	ISBN 978-7-5693-1754-1
定　　价	96.00元

读者购书、书店添货，如发现印装质量问题，请与本社发行中心联系、调换。
订购热线：（029）82665248　（029）82665249
投稿热线：（029）82668525

版权所有　侵权必究

《港之风帆》编委会

总策划：成　进
统　筹：李　重
主　编：李晓鸣　程洪莉
副主编：董　琪　朱建欣　刘鸿翔
编　委：谢霞宇　吴　丹　张雨金　温景涛　聂文信　吴　娜　李　玮　曹　琰　朱萍萍　毕晓楠
　　　　胡晓楠
摄　影：庄　稼　朱建欣　刘鸿翔　李一鸣　陈雪江　张　玥　尹承龙　郭小龙　卢　敏　孙金绒
　　　　白延生　邵晓民　罗　星　程国庆　侯　磊　梁星源　孙新建　王宜涛　朱翠兰　梁　骁
　　　　雷祥舒　臧绪丰　韩亚楼　问　炀　王晓凯　安　倩　范　波　邢　鹏　李　璐　张　杰
　　　　纪明彪　方彬任　@西域贤王等
书名题字：王　劲
装帧设计：董　琪　姚　瑶
出　品：西安交通大学党委宣传部
资料支持：西安交通大学工会　创新港办公室　国际处　科研院　社科处　实验室处　规建中心
　　　　学科办　共享实验中心　创新港发展公司　创新港实业公司　陕建集团

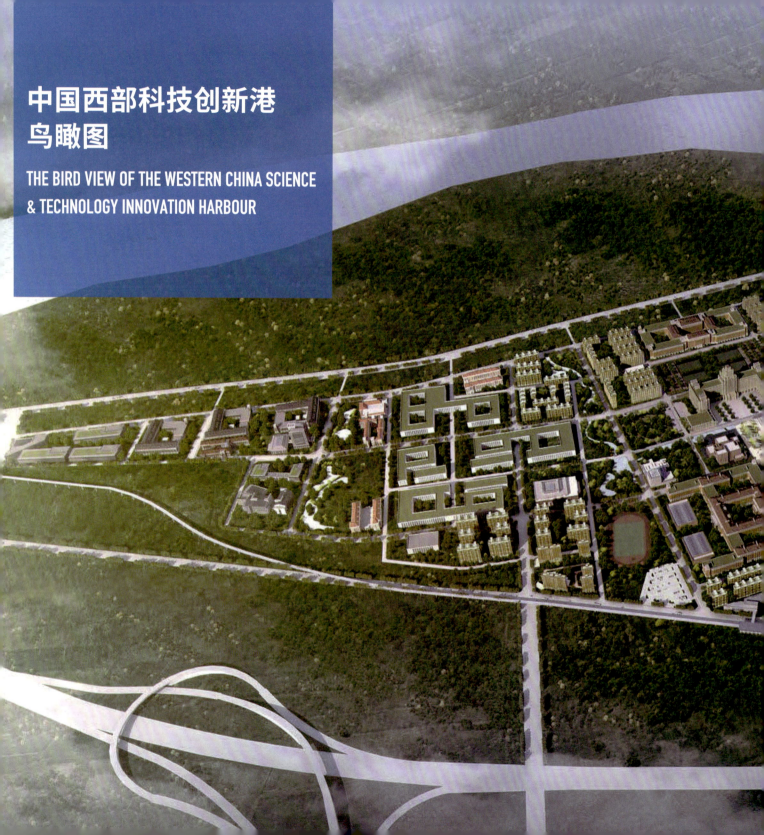

中国西部科技创新港
鸟瞰图

THE BIRD VIEW OF THE WESTERN CHINA SCIENCE
& TECHNOLOGY INNOVATION HARBOUR

前言

港之风帆

大船始出港
风劲好扬帆

1896年,南洋公学于沪上卓然而立,开创我国工程教育的源头,"兴学强国"的交大初心由此发轫。

1956年,交通大学响应党和国家号召内迁西安,吹响"向科学进军,建设大西北"的嘹亮号角,爱国奋斗的西迁精神孕育熔铸。

而今,西安交通大学再次"向西,向远方",打造创新重镇——中国西部科技创新港,以科技动力撬动西部发展,以开放包容助推"一带一路"国际合作。

俯瞰中国西部科技创新港,其形若大鹏,振翅翱翔。

这里,是陕西建设创新型省份,聚焦"追赶超越"目标,落实"五个扎实"要求的"新典范";

这里,是西安市深化统筹科技资源改革,加快推进全面创新改革试验区建设的"新样板";

这里,是西安交大深度融入国家发展大格局,探索中国特色世界一流大学建设的"新模式"。

中国西部科技创新港,火热书写科技引擎推动、合纵连横腾飞的创新梦想,人们将从这里读懂大学的未来。

中国西部科技创新港,引领时代发展,打造改革高地,人们也将从这里读懂未来的中国。

未来已来。一个世界级的科学研究高地正屹立于祖国西部,成为科技进步的驱动力、"一带一路"的创新源和西部发展的新引擎。

吞吐大荒,万象在旁,中国西部科技创新港,为世界之光!

PREFACE

The ship is going to sail while the wind is strong.

Nanyang Mission College, pioneer of engineering education in China, was established in Shanghai in 1896. Here the original intention of "building a strong country through education" was born. In 1956, under the call of the Communist Party of China and the country, Jiaotong University moved to Xi'an, answering the clarion call of "marching toward science and building the great northwest ". Today, Xi'an Jiaotong University (XJTU) is once again "moving west and moving further" to build the Western China Science & Technology Innovation Harbour, aiming at driving the development of western China with the power of science and technology, and boosting the international cooperation of the"Belt and Road Initiative" with openness and inclusiveness.

Overlooking iHarbour, we can see that its shape is like a roc, taking its wings and soaring. Here, iHarbour is a "big move" of national innovation-driven strategy, the western development layout, and the "Belt and Road Initiative" . Here, Shaanxi is building an innovative province, focusing on catching up and exceeding the goal, implementing the "new model" of "five solid" requirements. Here, a "new pilot zone" for Xi'an has been set up to deepen the reform of scientific and technological resources and accelerate the construction of comprehensive innovation. Here, a "new model" for XJTU to deeply integrate into the national development pattern and explore the construction of world-class university with Chinese characteristics is being set up.

iHarbour has been driven by science technology and people will understand the future of the university from here.iHarbour will lead the development of the times and create a highland for reform. People will also understand the future of China from here. A world-class scientific research highland is standing in the western China, becoming the driving force of scientific and technological progress, the innovation source of the "Belt and Road", and the new engine of western development of the country.

Grand and magnificent, the iHarbour is the light of the world!

CONTENTS

01.
大笔如椽
BIG ACTION

01

创新港,交大梦。从宏伟蓝图到跃然眼前,交大人以时不我待、只争朝夕的干劲成就了追风逐电的新时代交大速度。进驻创新港、勇攀新高峰已经成为交大师生奉献报国的新动能。

02.
海纳百川
INCLUSIVENESS

24

启动创新引擎,焕发改革活力。创新港大胆改革,在体制机制上涤故更新;主动承担国家重要任务,打造科技创新"蓄水池";汇聚全球智力资源,以海纳百川的胸襟开展国际交流合作。

03.
智慧学镇
THE SMART TOWN

52

创新港融入海绵城市、绿色建筑、装配式建筑、立体绿化、分布式能源等技术，建设集教育、科研、创业、生活为一体的智慧学镇，打造生态优先的绿色格局。

04.
生机盎然
VIGOUR & VITALITY

72

创新港扎根西部大地，一派生机盎然，以活力之港、现代之港、奋斗之港点亮创新火炬，成为莘莘学子向往的未来之港。

01.
大笔如椽
BIG ACTION

创新港，交大梦。从宏伟蓝图到跃然眼前，交大人以时不我待、只争朝夕的干劲成就了追风逐电的新时代交大速度。进驻创新港、勇攀新高峰已经成为交大师生奉献报国的新动能。

iHarbour is the dream of XJTU. Staffs and students of XJTU achieve the marvelous speed of new era with devotion and determination, turning the grand blueprint to the reality. Entering into iHarbour and climbing up mountain with great courage has bceome the new driven force of the staffs and students of XJTU.

国家使命担当
UNDERTAKING NATIONAL MISSION

中国西部科技创新港——智慧学镇是教育部和陕西省人民政府共建的国家级项目,由西安交通大学与陕西省西咸新区联合建设,选址于西咸新区沣西新城,建设用地规模约 5000 余亩。

The Western China Science and Technology Innovation Harbour—Smart Town is a national project co-administrated by Ministry of Education and Shaanxi Provincial People's Government. It is jointly built by XJTU and Xi Xian New Area of Shaanxi Province, located in Fengxi New Satellite City with over 3.33 km² building area.

区位优势
LOCATION ADVANTAGES

　　创新港北临渭河，位于新西宝高速线以北与新河三角洲交汇区域，规划建设面积约 3 平方公里。渭河、新河交织使创新港具备得天独厚的生态环境和优良的区位价值。公路、轨道、民航相互交融的大交通格局，为创新港搭建了功能完善的现代化综合运输体系，全面提升了创新港的辐射能力。

　　Next to the south of Weihe River, iHarbour is located at the intersection area between the new Xi'an-Baoji Expressway and Xinhe Delta in the north. The planned construction area is about 3 km². The interweaving of Weihe River and Xinhe River makes iHarbour an area possessing unique ecological environment and excellent location value. The traffic pattern of expressway, track and civil aviation intermingle with each other. A modern comprehensive transport system with perfect functions has been built for iHarbour, and the impact of iHarbour has been improved in an all round way.

六大目标
SIX GOALS

世界科学研究的中国特区

CHINA'S SPECIAL ZONE FOR WORLD SCIENTIFIC RESEARCH

人才培养和集聚的国际高地

AN INTERNATIONAL PLATFORM FOR TALENT CULTIVATING AND ABSORBING

国际化产学研协同创新基地

INNOVATION BASE OF INTERNATIONALIZED INDUSTRY-EDUCATION-RESEARCH COLLABORATION

高新技术企业成长的丝路硅谷

SILK ROAD SILICON VALLEY OF HIGH-TECH ENTERPRISES

新型城镇化的西部样板

WESTERN MODEL OF NEW URBANIZATION

科技教育资源统筹的示范城区

DEMONSTRATION CITY-ZONE OF SCIENCE AND TECHNOLOGY EDUCATION RESOURCES SYNERGY

创新驱动平台
INNOVATION-DRIVEN PLATFORM

创新港建设"校区、园区、社区"三位一体的创新体、技术与服务的结合体、科技与产业的融合体，打造高等教育综合改革的交大样板、新型城镇化的西咸典范和科技创新的国家级示范区。

iHarbour is built as an innovative complex of campus, park and community, a combination of technology and service and a joint industry of science, technology, as well as a sample of comprehensive reform of higher education Xi Xian model of new urbanization and a national demonstration area of the science and technology innovation.

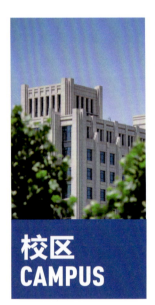

校区 CAMPUS

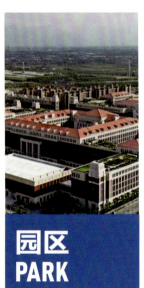

园区 PARK

社区 COMMUNITY

智慧学镇示范
EXEMPLARY SMART TOWN

　　创新港将现代田园城市理念与国际著名高校"学镇"校园规划理念相结合，打造生态友好、环境宜居、开放包容、青春激扬的魅力家园。

　　iHarbour combines the concept of modern garden city with the campus planning concept of "smart town" of internationally renowned universities to create a charming home with ecological friendliness, livable environment, openness and inclusiveness, and vigorous youth.

全球科教高地
HIGHLANDS OF GLOBAL SCIENCE & EDUCATION

创新港创造性提出科研巨构群的形态，促进多学科交叉融合，为打破学科壁垒、开辟交叉学科研究领域、培养高端创新人才厚植土壤，打造科技创新重地。

iHarbour creatively puts forward the form of giant scientific research group, promotes the interdisciplinary integration, breaks through disciplinary barriers, opens up interdisciplinary research fields, cultivates high-level and innovative talents, and builds an important platform for scientific and technological innovations.

服务陕西引擎
DRIVING FORCE OF SHAANXI PROVINCE

　　创新港充分发挥大学在创新驱动陕西区域经济发展中的"源头创新"作用,推动陕西科技创新走在前列,助力陕西发展"追赶超越"。

　　iHarbour takes the lead in the innovation-driven economic development in Shaanxi Province,and helps the province to "catch up and surpass" other devel- oped provinces and regions.

传承交大文脉
INHERITANCE & DELIVERY OF XJTU'S SPIRIT

创新港建筑传承交大文脉，以中轴线对称为布局，以坡屋顶的红色为色基，"饮水思源"的交大传统在创新港建筑中得到了淋漓尽致的体现。

The constructions in iHarbour inherit the great tradition of XJTU with symmetrical central axis as layout, red sloping roofs as colour base. The tradition of "gratitude for the source of benefit" is vividly reflected.

融入社会发展
INTEGRATING INTO SOCIAL DEVELOPMENT

创新港打破大学与社会的壁垒，与城市完美融合，着力打造"没有围墙的大学"。

iHarbour sets up no walls between university and the outside world, perfectly blending into the society. It strives to build a "university without walls".

缔造交大速度
XJTU'S SPEED

创新港科创基地自破土动工至全面封顶，历时 8 个月，生动诠释了新时期的"交大速度"。

It only takes 8 months for XJTU to complete the construction of the Science & Technology Innovation Base from scratch. Through it, "XJTU's speed" of the new era can be vividly observed.

2019年6月
创新港科创基地
一期交付点亮

PHASE, I DELIVERY & LIGHTING OF
THE SCIENCE & TECHNOLOGY INNOVATION
BASE IN IHARBOUR, JUNE 2019

2019年9月
创新港新生开学典礼

OPENING CEREMONY FOR
GRADUATE STUDENTS IN
IHARBOUR
SEPTEMBER 2019

02.
海纳百川
INCLUSIVENESS

启动创新引擎，焕发改革活力。创新港大胆改革，在体制机制上涤故更新；主动承担国家重要任务，打造科技创新"蓄水池"；汇聚全球智力资源，以海纳百川的胸襟开展国际交流合作。

Driven by innovation and reform, iHarbour takes a giant step in reformation; in system and mechanism, XJTU starts over; besides, we take the initiative to undertake the key national tasks and create a "reservoir" of scientific and technological innovation. We also gather global intellectual resources to carry out international exchanges and cooperation with open mind.

瞄准国家战略
TARGETING NATIONAL STRATEGY

创新港瞄准国家战略方向，开展前沿问题探索和关键技术攻关，努力推动关键技术转变为先进生产力。

iHarbour aims at the national strategy, tackles with cutting-edge issues and key technology, striving to promote the transformation of key technologies into advanced productive forces.

能源革命 ENERGY REVOLUTION
- 新能源 NEW ENERGY
- 新材料 NEW MATERIALS
- 装备制造 EQUIPMENT MANUFACTURE

中国制造2025 MADE IN CHINA 2025
- 生态环保 ECOLOGICAL & ENVIRONMENTAL PROTECTION
- 生物医药 BIOLOGICAL MEDICINE
- 高端智库 TOP THINK TANKS

互联网+ INTERNET +
- 大数据 BIG DATA
- 人工智能 ARTIFICIAL INTELLIGENCE
- 电力装备 ELECTRIC POWER EQUIPMENT

健康中国 HEALTH CHINA
- 基础科学 BASIC SCIENCE
- 航空航天 AERONAUTICS AND ASTRONAUTICS
- 化学化工 CHEMISTRY AND CHEMICAL ENGINEERING

打造科技高地
CREATING A HIGHLAND FOR SCIENCE AND TECHNOLOGY

港是开放的，创新港乃科技资源"吞吐"之港。"吞"即借鉴国内外先进经验与模式，整合创新资源，吸引海内外科技资源和科技人才，进行科学试验、技术成果转化及创新；"吐"则是发挥自主创新能力，将优质的科技成果、创新产品、高素质人才等源源不断地向社会输出。创新港规划科研、教育、转孵化、综合配套四大板块，同时积极谋划在南侧西咸新区、北侧咸阳高新区建设产业承载区，以进一步扩大创新港的辐射作用，承接创新港产生的科研成果并实现就地转化。

iHarbour is open. It is the place where the scientific and technological resources are imported and exported simutaneously. To import means to learn from the advanced experiences and modes from home and abroad, integrate various innovative resources and talents, carry out scientific experiments, transform and innovate technological achievements. To export is to give full play to the independent innovation, and continuously make high-quality scientific and technological achievements, produce innovative products and train quality talents. iHarbour is planned to have four major sections: Scientific Research Section, Education Section, Incubation Section and Integrated Service Section. At the same time, the University is building the industrial supporting zone in the Xi Xian New Area and Xianyang Hi-tech Industries Development Zone, so as to further expand the impact role of iHarbour.

科研板块
SCIENTIFIC RESEARCH

围绕理、工、文、医四大板块，布局建设一批研究院及研究所(中心)。

Building scientific, institutions(centers) in the field of science, engineering,medicine and art.

教育板块
EDUCATION

12000 余名研究生、近 1000名留学生、50000 名高素质人才汇集。

More than 12,000 graduate students, almost 1,000 overseas students, 50,000 high-quality talents.

转孵化板块
INCUBATION

孵化器、加速器、中试厂房、联合实验室、服务设施及机构。

Incubator, accelerator, pilot plant, joint laboratory, service facilities and institutions.

综合服务配套板块
INTEGRATED SERVICE

中学、小学、幼儿园、医院和医养社区、配套商业、专家公寓、文化体育设施。

Affiliated schools and kindergardens, hospital, medical care communities, businesses, expert apartments, cultural and sports facilities.

创新港科创基地
（科研、教育板块）
SCIENCE AND TECHNOLOGY INNOVATION BASE

科创基地一期主要建设科研、教育相关建筑 52 栋，占地约 1625 亩，总建筑面积 160 万平方米。科创基地二期主要建设中国西部先进核能技术研究院、文化图书中心等，占地约 625 亩，总建筑面积约 40 万平方米。

There are 52 buildings for scientific research and education of the first phase of Science & Technology Innovation Base, covering an area of about 1,080,000 m², with a total construction area of 1.6 million m². The phase II of the project covers an area of about 41,000 m² and a total building area of about 400,000 m² including Western China Institute of Advanced Nuclear Energy Technology, Culture and Book Center and so on.

29 个
研究院 / 中心
29 RESEARCH INSTITUTES/ CENTERS

29 个
国家级科研基地
29 NATIONAL SCIENTIFIC RESEARCH BASES

42 个
人文社科重点研究基地及智库
42 HUMANITIES AND SOCIAL SCIENCE KEY RESEARCH BASES AND THINK TANKS

128 个
省部级重点科研基地
128 PROVINCIAL KEY SCIENTIFIC RESEARCH BASES

30 个
博士后科研流动站
30 CENTERS FOR POST-DOCTORAL STUDIES

6 个
大型仪器设备公共平台
6 LARGE INSTRUMENT AND EQUIPMENT COLLABORATION PLATFORMS

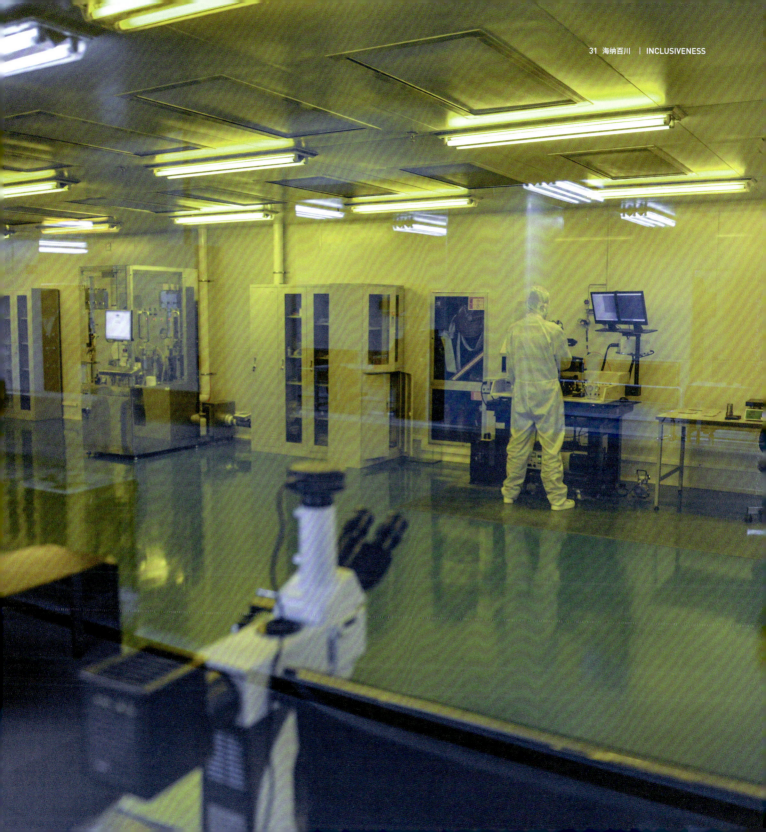

启动创新引擎
LAUNCHING INNOVATION ENGINE

创新港面向国家重大需求建设 29 个研究院，重点解决影响国计民生的卡脖子技术问题、行业关键核心技术问题等。

iHarbour has 29 research institutes to meet the country's major needs, focusing on solving problems affecting people's livelihood and core technologies in the industry.

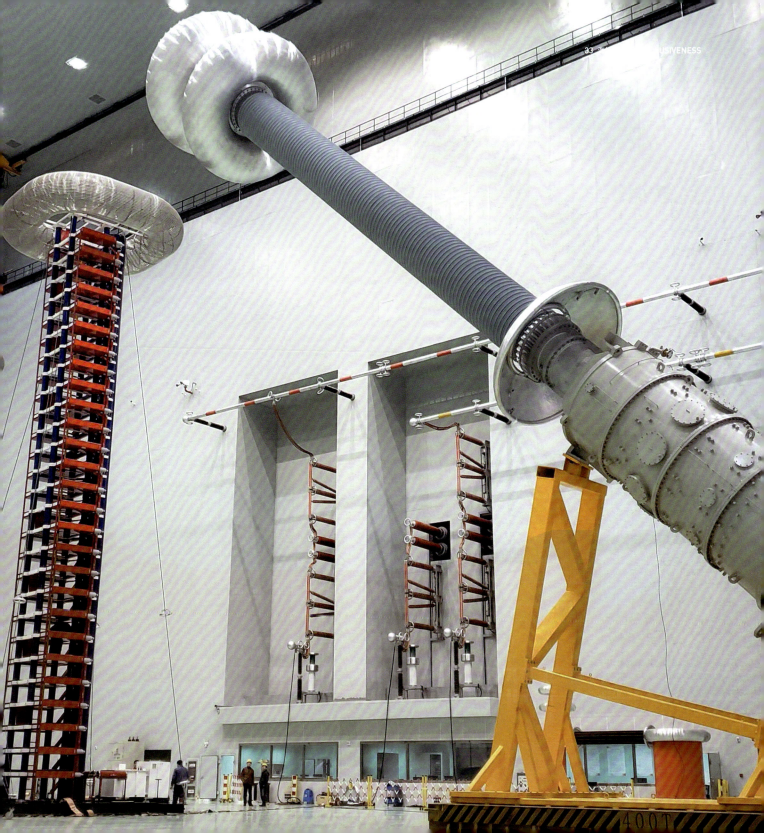

建设重大平台
BUILDING KEY PLATFORMS

探索科学现象，引领科技革命，打造国际前沿的科学研究体系，一批探索未来的科学中心落户创新港，围绕新能源、装备制造等"卡脖子"难题开展科技攻关，彰显创新港使命担当。

A number of scientific centers that explore scientific phenomena, lead the scientific and technological revolution, and build the international cutting-edge scientific research system have settled in the iHarbour. Platforms such as state key laboratories are demonstrating the mission of the iHarbour.

动力工程多相流国家重点实验室
STATE KEY LABORATORY OF MULTIPHASE FLOW IN POWER ENGINEERING

金属材料强度国家重点实验室
STATE KEY LABORATORY FOR MECHANICAL BEHAVIOR OF METERIALS

电力设备电气绝缘国家重点实验室
STATE KEY LABORATORY OF ELECTRICAL INSULATION AND POWER EQUIPMENT

机械制造系统工程国家重点实验室
STATE KEY LABORATORY FOR MANUFACTURING SYSTEMS ENGINEERING

机械结构强度与振动国家重点实验室
STATE KEY LABORATORY FOR STRENGTH AND VIBRATION OF MECHANICAL STRUCTURES

快速制造国家工程研究中心
NATIONAL ENGINEERING RESEARCH CENTER OF RAPID MANUFACTURING

流体机械及压缩机国家工程研究中心
NATIONAL ENGINEERING RESEARCH CENTER OF FLUID MACHINERY AND COMPRESSORS

视觉信息处理与应用国家工程实验室
NATIONAL ENGINEERING LABORATORY FOR VISUAL INFORMATION PROCESSING AND APPLICATIONS

大数据算法与分析技术国家工程实验室
NATIONAL ENGINEERING LABORATORY FOR BIG DATA ANALYTICS

35 海纳百川 | INCLUSIVENESS

践行"四个面向"
PRACTICE "FOUR ORIENTATIONS"

以"四个面向"为引领，发挥创新港辐射带动作用，在原有科技平台基础上，构建重大科技基础设施群和重大科技创新平台群，打造重要的科研与文教中心。

Guided by "Four Orientations", iHarbour, relying on its initial science and technology platform, should play the leading role in building infrastructure and innovation platform of major science and technology and center of major science research, culture and education.

大科学装置
LARGE RESEARCH INFRASTRUCTURES

Z 箍缩及应用重大科技基础设施（筹）
Major Science And Technology Infrastructure Of Z-Pinch (In Preparation)

宏微纳跨尺度基标准重大科技基础设施（筹）
Major Science And Technology Infrastructure Of Macro, Micro And Nano Multi-scale Standards (In Preparation)

航空发动机结构服役安全试验重大科技基础设施（筹）
Major Science And Technology Infrastructure Of Safety Test Of Aeroengine Structure In Service (In Preparation)

重型燃气轮机高温强度与质量控制平台（筹）
Control Platform Of High-temperature Strength And Quality Of Heavy Duty Gas Turbine (In Preparation)

多用途静默式核电源（筹）
Multifunctional Silent Nuclear Power Battery (In Preparation)

钠冷快堆核心关键设备蒸汽发生器实验平台
Steam Generator Experimental Platform For Key Equipment Of Sodium-cooled Fast Reactor

装备制造
EQUIPMENT MANUFACTURE

中国西部质量科学技术研究院
Western China Scientific and Technological Research Institute of Quality

爆震发动机平台（筹）
Detonation Engine Platform (In Preparation)

人工智能与大数据
ARTIFICIAL INTELLIGENCE AND BIG DATA

陕西国家应用数学中心
National Center for Applied Mathematics

人工智能研究中心（筹）
Artificial Intelligence Research Center (In Preparation)

生命医学
LIFE AND MEDICAL SCIENCE

区域医疗中心（筹）
Regional Medical Center (In Preparation)

区域大型仪器设备共享中心（筹）
Regional Core Facility Sharing Center (In Preparation)

实验动物中心（筹）
Laboratory Animal Center (In Preparation)

能源
ENERGY

国家西部能源研究院
National West Energy Research Institute

先进电力能源科学技术研究院
Scientific and Technological Research Institute of Advanced Electrical Energy

中国西部先进核能技术研究院
Advanced Nuclear Power Research Institute of Western China

人文社科
HUMANITIES AND SOCIAL SCIENCE

传播内容认知国家重点实验室
National Key Laboratory of Communication Contents Cognition

社会治理与经济发展大数据智能化分析集成平台（筹）
Intelligent Big Data Analysis and Integration Platform for Social Governance and Economic Growth (In Preparation)

"一带一路"暨"上合组织"国际化创新研究平台（筹）
International Innovation Research Platform of "The Belt and Road Initiative" and "Shanghai Cooperation Organization" (In Preparation)

融入"一带一路"
INTEGRATING INTO THE "BELT AND ROAD INITIATIVE"

创新港国际化平台凸显"一体两翼"战略,即以提升学校国际影响力、竞争力为"本体",以建设丝绸之路大学联盟和推进与一流大学合作为"两翼",提升学校在世界高等教育领域的话语权和影响力。丝绸之路大学联盟目前已吸引37个国家和地区的150余所大学加盟,打造"一带一路"高等教育"朋友圈"。

The international platform of the iHabour highlights the strategy of "One Body, Two Wings" in which "One Body" means enhancing the international influence and competitiveness of XJTU, and "Two Wings" refers to building the "University Alliance of the Silk Road (UASR)" and promoting cooperation with first-class universities, with the aim of enhancing the voice and influence of XJTU in higher education. UASR has now attracted more than 150 universities from 37 countries and regions to build a "Belt and Road" higher education circle.

39 海纳百川 | INCLUSIVENESS

拓展国际合作
EXPANDING INTERNATIONAL COOPERATION

西安交通大学与 45 个国家和地区的逾 320 所高校和研究机构建立了校际合作关系，许多合作伙伴纷纷向创新港伸出橄榄枝，这里已经成为开放合作的最前沿。在创新港，西安交通大学与意大利米兰理工大学共建联合设计学院，与澳大利亚新南威尔士大学、英国伯明翰大学等合作组建微纳制造与测试技术国际合作联合实验室，与美国明尼苏达大学建立热科学与工程国际合作联合实验室，与美国杰克逊实验室联合建立精准医学研究中心，与德国于利希研究中心等积极探索人才培养和科研合作新模式。

XJTU has established inter-campus cooperation with more than 320 universities and research institutes in 45 countries and regions. Many partners are willing to extend an olive branch to the Harbour, which will become the forefront place of open cooperation. In the Harbour, XJTU and Polytechnic University of Milan in Italy jointly built XJTU-POLIMI Joint School of Design. XJTU cooperated with the University of New South Wales in Australia and Birmingham University in the United Kingdom to set up the Joint Laboratory for International Cooperation in Micro-nano Manufacturing and Testing Technology. XJTU also set up the Joint Laboratory for International Cooperation in Thermal Science and Engineering and a Research Center for Precision Medicine with the University of Minnesota and Jackson Laboratory in the United States respectively. XJTU actively explored new models of personnel training and scientific research cooperation with Forschungszentrum Jülich, Germany.

勇当科技先锋
PIONEER IN SCIENCE AND TECHNOLOGY

创新港翻开政产学研合作新篇章：与商务部、陕西省人民政府共建"丝绸之路经济带法律政策协同创新中心"，首倡"丝绸之路学术带"；与国家发展改革委共同建设"改革试点探索与评估协同创新中心"；与陕西省自贸办联合成立"一带一路"自由贸易试验区研究院，标志着西部自贸试验区研究工作进入国际化、市场化、开放式的新阶段；与中国核工业集团有限公司共建中国西部先进核能技术研究院，加快推进军民融合战略，助推我国核工业创新发展；与香港中文大学组建人口迁移联合研究中心；与陕西省土地工程建设集团共建土地工程与人居环境技术创新中心等。

iHarbour opens a new chapter of the cooperation among the government, industry, education and research: XJTU, with the Ministry of Commerce and Shaanxi Provincial People's Government, has established the "Silk Road Economic Belt Legal Policy Synergy Innovation Center" and initiated the "Silk Road Academic Belt". XJTU and the National Development and Reform Commission jointly established the "Innovation Center of China Economic Reform Pilot and Assessment"; and with the Shaanxi Free Trade Zone Office, the University has established XJTU Institute of " The Belt And The Road" Pilot Free Trade Zone. The institute marks a new stage of internationalization, marketization and openness in the research work of the Western Free Trade Zone. Together with China Nuclear Industry Group Co., Ltd., XJTU established the Western China Institute of Advanced Nuclear Energy Technology to accelerate the strategy of civil-military integration and promote the innovative development of China's nuclear industry. XJTU and the Chinese University of Hong Kong jointly built XJTU-CUHK Joint Research Center on Migration. XJTU and Shaanxi Provincial Land Engineering Construction Group co-established the Technical Innovation Center of Land Engineering and Human Settlements Environment.

"一带一路"自由贸易试验区研究院
XJTU INSTITUTE OF "THE BELT AND THE ROAD" PILOT FREE TRADE ZONE

改革试点探索与评估协同创新中心
COLLABORATIVE INNOVATION CENTER OF CHINA PILOT REFORM EXXPLORATION AND ASSESSMENT

丝绸之路经济带法律政策协同创新中心
COLLABORATIVE INNOVATION CENTRE FOR SILK ROAD ECONOMIC BELT LEGAL AND POLICY STUDIES

中国西部先进核能技术研究院
WESTERN CHINA INSTITUTE OF ADVANCED NUCLEAR ENERGY TECHNOLOGY

土地工程与人居环境技术创新中心
TECHNOLOGICAL INNOVATION CENTER OF LAND ENGINEERING AND HUMAN SETTLEMENTS

人口迁移联合研究中心
XJTU-CUHK JOINT RESEARCH CENTER ON MIGRATION

43. 海纳百川 | INCLUSIVENESS

汇聚天下英才
ATTRACTING TALENTS
FROM ALL OVER THE WORLD

创新港坚持自主培养与积极吸引创新型人才相结合，打造人才培养和集聚的国际高地。2019 年 4 月 2 日，中国西部海外博士后创新示范中心进驻创新港，致力打造中国西部高等教育"智高点"。

iHarbour insists on the combination of independent training and actively attracting innovative talents to create an international highland for talents training and gathering. On April 2, 2019, Western China Overseas Postdoctoral Innovation Demonstration Center of Western China entered into iHarbour to build the "Intellectual Highland" of higher education in Western China.

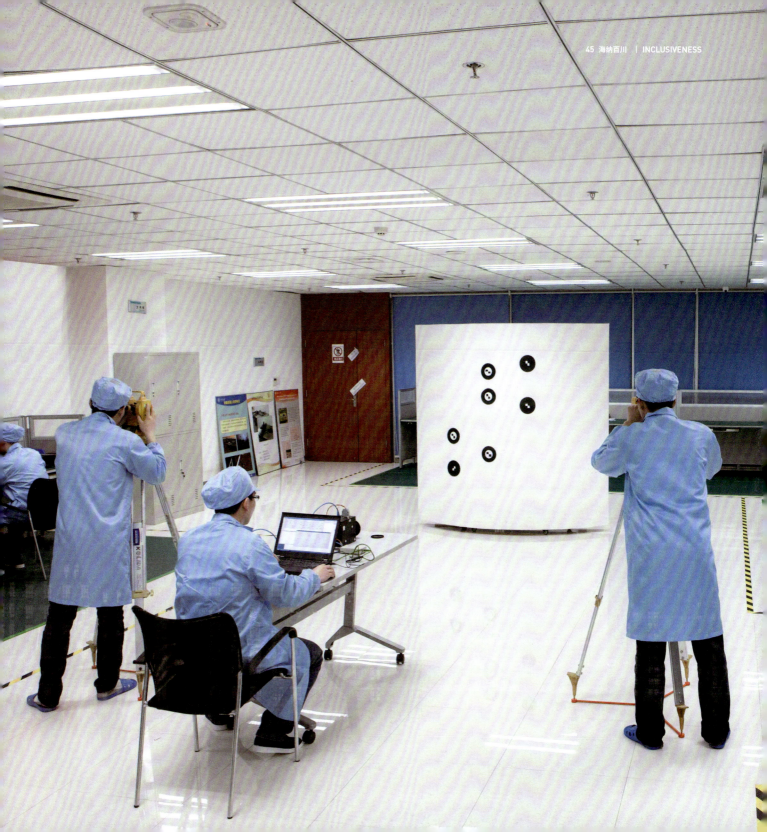

45　海纳百川　| INCLUSIVENESS

优化共享平台
OPTIMIZING SHARING PLATFORM

创新港整合优质设备资源,创新运行管理机制,落实开放共享政策,提升资源使用效益,设立大型仪器设备公共平台,有力支撑区域发展与产业技术研发。

iHarbour integrates high-quality equipment, innovates operation and management mechanism, implements the policy of opening and sharing, and enhances the efficiency of resource utilization through setting up large instrument and equipment collalooration platform so as to support the regional development and industrial technological research and production.

大型仪器设备共享实验中心
CORE FACILITIES AND EXPERIMENT CENTER

- 分析测试中心 INSTRUMENTAL ANALYSIS CENTER
- 高性能计算中心 HIGH PERFORMANCE COMPUTING CENTER
- 微纳电子器件实验中心 EXPERIMENTAL CENTER FOR MICRO/NANO ELECTRONIC DEVICES
- 实验动物中心 LABORATORY ANIMAL CENTER
- 生物医学实验中心 EXPERIMENTAL CENTER OF BIOLOGY AND MEDICINE
- 微纳制造中心 MICRO- AND NANO - MANUFACTURING RESEARCH CENTER

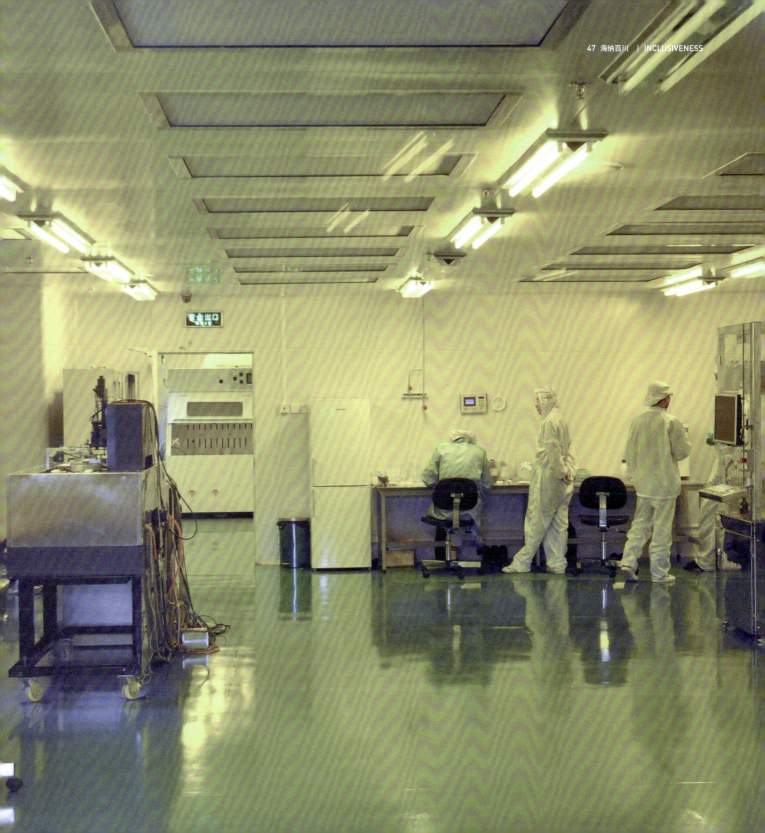

深化产教融合
DEEPENING THE INTEGRATION OF INDUSTRY AND EDUCATION

创新港先行先试、破题示范，深化产教融合，加速推进"6352"工程，打造构建科技成果转化特区、"两链"融合示范区和国际创新高地。

The Innovation Harbour takes the lead in the pilot project of integrating industry and education to step up the implementation of Project "6352" so as to open up a special zone for commercialization of research achievements, and to build a demonstration area for the integration of innovation chain and industrial chain and an international stronghold for innovation. Specifically, Project "6352" refers to the following:

49 海纳百川 | INCLUSIVENESS

推进协同育人
PROMOTING COLLABORATIVE EDUCATION

2021年4月8日,"产教融合、协同育人"创新工程启动大会在创新港举行,现代产业学院、未来技术学院正式揭牌。现代产业学院致力于加强校企深度融合,与企业共同探索校企联合科研攻关与协同育人新范式,构建完善以科技创新和实际应用为导向的复合型高层次创新人才培养体系。未来技术学院致力于面向未来五年的前沿性、革命性、颠覆性的新方向、新专业、新学科,实现未来技术创新突破和拔尖人才培养。

On April 8, 2021,The conference for launching Project "6352" was held at iHarbour campus with "Integration of Industry and Education, Collaboration in Student Education" as the slogan, the School of Modern Industry and the School of Emerging Technologies were officially unveiled. The School of Modern Industry is committed to strengthening the deep integration of the school and enterprises, exploring new models of joint research between the school and enterprises and collaborative education with enterprises, and constructing a comprehensive high-level innovative student education system oriented on science and technology innovation and practical applications. The School of Emerging Technologies is committed to the frontier, revolutionary, and trail-blazing new research areas, new majors, new disciplines towards the next five years so as to achieve technological innovation breakthroughs and top-notch talent training.

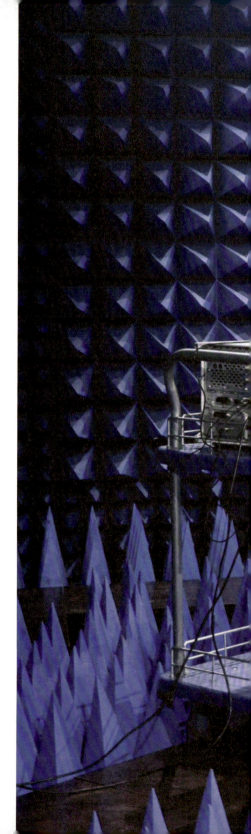

03.
智慧学镇
THE SMART TOWN

创新港融入海绵城市、绿色建筑、装配式建筑、立体绿化、分布式能源等技术，建设集教育、科研、创业、生活为一体的智慧学镇，打造生态优先的绿色格局。

iHarbour integrates sponge city, green building, prefabricated building, three-dimensional greening, distributed energy and other technologies, building a smart town integrating education, scientific research, entrepreneurship and life, and creating a green pattern with ecological priority.

生态新港
ECO-INNOVATION HARBOUR

创新港北临渭河，东有沙河，西为涝河，水野拥城，生态宜人。

iHarbour faces Weihe River in the north, Shahe River in the east, Laohe River in the west. The campus is surrounded with water and grass. It is ecologically pleasant.

港之风帆 56

57 智慧学镇 | THE SMART TOWN

宜居家园
LIVABLE HOME

创新港建设高端人才生活基地，面积从 90 平方米到 300 平方米，满足不同人才的不同需求。

iHarbour builds a high-end talent living base, covering an area of 90 m² to 300 m², to meet different needs of talents.

海绵城市
SPONGE CITY

雨水在创新港自然积存、自然渗透和自然净化,实现可持续水循环。

The technology of natural accumulation, natural infiltration and natural purification of rainwater in iHarbour makes sustainable water circulation possible.

63 智慧学镇 | THE SMART TOWN

绿色建筑
GREEN BUILDING

创新港建筑严格按照节能标准设计，其围护结构采用新技术、新材料、新标准，降低建筑物能耗。屋顶花园四季常绿，三季有花。

All the buildings in iHarbour are designed strictly according to the energy-saving standard. Their envelope structure adopts new technologies, new materials and new standards to reduce building energy consumption. The roof gardens have flowers all year round.

5G校园
5G CAMPUS

创新港依托 5G 技术，孵化有力支撑教学科研、能源管理、安全保障和生活服务的智能化校园服务体系，构建全国首个智慧学镇 5G 校园。

iHarbour relies on 5G technology, incubates an intelligent campus service system that strongly supports teaching and research, energy management, security and life services. It is the first 5G campus of smart town in China.

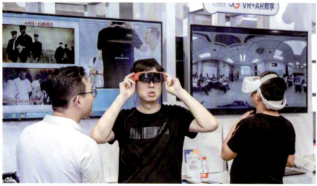

04.
生机盎然
VIGOUR & VITALITY

创新港扎根西部大地,一派生机盎然,以活力之港、现代之港、奋斗之港点亮创新火炬,成为莘莘学子向往的未来之港。

iHarbour takes root in the western China and is full of vitality. It lights the torch of innovation with vigour, modernness and striving. It is the ideal harbour that countless students yearn for.

广阔学习空间
WIDE LEARNING SPACE

创新港拥有广阔的学习空间，可同时容纳8000余名学子上课，多种形式的研讨室可容纳近万名学子碰撞思想火花。

iHarbour offers a wide space for learning. It can accommodate more than 8,000 students for classes at the same time. The seminar rooms of various forms can accommodate nearly 10,000 students for the collision of ideas.

新型住宿社区
NEW STUDENT APARTMENTS

创新港公寓格局为五室一厅，单人单间，共享客厅。三个住宿区共有 34 栋公寓楼，16438 间宿舍。

There are 34 apartment buildings and 16,438 dormitories in the three residential areas, with five private rooms and one living room in each apartment. One student lives in a private room; he/she shares the living room with other four students.

便利校园生活
CONVENIENT CAMPUS LIFE

创新港设有惠风苑、朗清苑、和鸣苑三座餐厅，博物馆、阅览中心、三甲医院、商业中心等一应俱全。

iHarbour has three canteens, namely Huifeng Canteen, Langqing Canteen and Heming Canteen, and it has Museum, Reading Center, Grade III Level A Hospital and Shopping Center.

85 生机盎然 | VIGOUR & VITALITY

HELLO,
创新港！

来创新港，在河滩上踢足球，湿地里喝咖啡，森林里做研究。

Playing football on the river beach, drinking coffee on the wetland, doing research in the forest, iHarbour is open to you!

HELLO,
创新港！

童心看世界，童画绘新港，交小苗与创新港一起长大。

Seeing the world from children's eyes and painting iHarbour with children's hands.

93 生机盎然 | VIGOUR & VITALITY

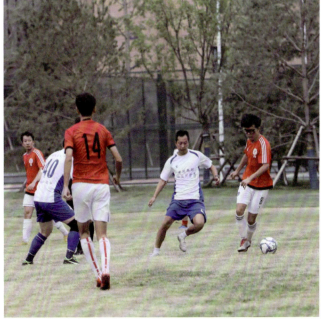

从创新港，扬帆起航！
STARTING FROM iHARBOUR!

创新港科创基地
THE TECHNOLOGY & SCIENCE INNOVATION BASE

敏行楼* MIN XING BUILDING 1号巨构

动力工程多相流国家重点实验室
STATE KEY LABORATORY OF MULTIPHASE FLOW IN POWER ENGINEERING

能源科学与技术研究院
INSTITUTE OF ENERGY SCIENCE AND TECHNOLOGY

新媒体与社会治理研究院
INSTITUTE OF NEW MEDIA AND SOCIAL GOVERNANCE

力行楼* LI XING BUILDING 2号巨构

机械制造系统工程国家重点实验室
STATE KEY LABORATORY FOR MANUFACTURING SYSTEM ENGINEER

机械结构强度与振动国家重点实验室
STATE KEY LABORATORY FOR STRENGTH AND VIBRATION OF MECHANICAL STRUCTURES

高端装备研究院
ACADEMY OF FRONTIER EQUIPMENT

空天与力学研究院
INSTITUTE OF AEROSPACE AND MECHANICS

微纳制造中心
MICRO-AND NANO-MANUFACTURING RESEARCH CENTER

躬行楼* GONG XING BUILDING 3号巨构

金属材料强度国家重点实验室
STATE KEY LABORATORY FOR MECHANICAL BEHAVIOR OF MATERIALS

电力设备电气绝缘国家重点实验室
STATE KEY LABORATORY OF ELECTRICAL INSTITUTION AND POWER EQUIPMENT

Z 箍缩及应用重大科技基础设施
SCIENCE CENTER OF Z-PINCH FACILITY

电气科学与技术研究院
INSTITUTE OF ELECTRICAL SCIENCE AND TECHNOLOGY

材料科学与工程研究院
INSTITUTE OF MATERIALS SCIENCE AND ENGINEERING

泓理楼* HONG LI BUILDING 4号巨构

电子信息科学研究院
INSTITUTE OF ELECTRICAL AND INFORMATION SCIENCE

物理科学与技术研究院
ACADEMY OF PHYSICAL SCIENCE AND TECHNOLOGY

西安数学与数学技术研究院
XI'AN INTERNATIONAL ACADEMY FOR MATHEMATICS AND METHEMATICAL TECHNOLOGY

高性能计算中心
CENTER FOR HIGH PERFORMANCE COMPUTING

微纳电子器件实验中心
EXPERIMENTAL CENTER FOR MICRO / NANO ELECTRONIC DEVICES

泓润楼* HONG RUN BUILDING 19号楼

化学工程与技术研究院
INSTITUTE OF CHEMICAL ENGINEERING AND TECHNOLOGY

化学研究院
ACADEMY OF CHEMISTRY

人居环境与建筑工程研究院(地球环境部分、土木部分)
INSTITUTE OF HUMAN SETTLEMENTS AND CIVIL ENGINEERING (GLOBAL ENVIRONMENT&CONSTRUCTION)

能源科学与技术研究院(环境部分)
INSTITUTE OF ENERGY SCIENCE ANDTECHNOLOGY

源居楼* YUAN JU BUILDING 7号楼

人居环境与建筑工程研究院(建筑学部分)
INSTITUTE OF HUMAN SETTLEMENTS AND CIVIL ENGINEERING (ARCHITECTURE)

泓生楼* HONG SHENG BUILDING 18号楼

生物医学与健康工程研究院
INSTITUTES OF BIOMEDICAL AND HEALTH ENGINEERING

分析测试共享中心
INSTRUMENTAL ANALYSIS CENTER

涵英楼* HAN YING BUILDING 5号楼

丝绸之路大学联盟
UNIVERSITY ALLIANCE OF THE SILK ROAD

中国西部海外博士后创新示范中心
WESTERN CHINA OVERSEAS POSTDOC INNOVATION DEMONSTRATION CENTER

"一带一路"自贸区研究院
XJTU INSTITUTE OF "THE BELT AND THE ROAD" PILOT FREE TRADE ZONE

文科高等研究院
ADVANCED INSTITUTE OF ARTS

管理研究院
MANAGEMENT RESEARCH INSTITUTE

经济金融研究院
INSTITUTE OF ECONOMICS AND FINANCE

公共政策与发展研究院
INSTITUTE OF PUBLIC POLICY AND DEVELOPMENT

人文与社会科学研究院
ACADEMY OF HUMANITIES AND SOCIAL SCIENCE

法学研究院
ACADEMY OF LAW

马克思主义与治国理政研究院
INSTITUTE OF MARXISM AND GOVERNANCE

语言文化及国际交流研究中心
CENTER FOR INTERNATIONAL STUDIES

金禾经济研究中心
JINHE CENTER FOR ECONOMIC RESEARCH

泓仁楼* HONG REN BUILDING 21号楼

转化医学研究院
TRANSLATIONAL MEDICINE INSTITUTE

Med-X 研究院
MED-X INSTITUTE

精准医疗研究院
PRECISION MEDICAL INSTITUTE

全球健康研究院
GLOBAL HEALTH INSTITUTE

生物证据研究院
FORENSIC BIOEVIDENCE INSTITUTE

药物科学与技术研究院
INSTITUTE OF PHARMACEUTICAL SCIENCE AND TECHNOLOGY

生物医学实验中心
BIOMEDICAL EXPERIMENTAL CENTER

米兰楼* MILAN BUILDING 6号楼

西安交大—米兰理工联合设计学院
XJTU-POLIMI JOINT SCHOOL OF DESIGN

西安交大—米兰理工联合创新中心
XJTU-POLIMI JOINT INNOVATION CENTRE

实验动物中心* LABORATORY ANIMAL CENTER 22号楼

阅览中心* READING CENTER 9号楼

中国西部先进核能技术研究院*
WESTERN CHINA INSTITUTE OF ADVANCED NUCLEAR ENERGY TECHNOLOGY

博物馆* MUSEUM 8号楼

联系创新港
CONTACTS

序号	研究院名称	所在学院(部)	联系人	邮箱
1	高端装备研究院	机械工程学院	张新功	xgzhang@xjtu.edu.cn
2	电气科学与技术研究院	电气工程学院	王 超	wcxjtu@163.com
3	能源科学与技术研究院	能源与动力工程学院	刘 佳	liujia@xjtu.edu.cn
4	电子信息科学研究院	电子与信息学部	李玉龙	liyulong@xjtu.edu.cn
5	材料科学与工程研究院	材料科学与工程学院	李 杰	huanhuan@xjtu.edu.cn
6	人居环境与建筑工程研究院	人居环境与建筑工程学院	孟祥兆	xzmeng@xjtu.edu.cn
7	生物医学与健康工程研究院	生命科学与技术学院	张 瑞	zrxajt@xjtu.edu.cn
8	空天与力学研究院	航天航空学院	车春莉	cheche@xjtu.edu.cn
9	化学工程与技术研究院	化学工程与技术学院	蔡元汉	caiyuanhan@xjtu.edu.cn
10	物理科学与技术研究院	物理学院	魏小平	weixiaoping@xjtu.edu.cn
11	化学研究院	化学学院	马瑞峰	marf@xjtu.edu.cn
12	西安数学与数学技术研究院	数学与统计学院	刘晓瑞	kuliguo@xjtu.edu.cn
13	Med-X研究院	医学部	佘军军	jessie_renhui@aliyun.com
14	精准医疗研究院	医学部	纪泛扑	jifanpu1979@163.com
15	全球健康研究院	医学部	闫立华	ylihua@xjtu.edu.cn
16	生物证据研究院	医学部	李 涛	litao050428@xjtu.edu.cn
17	药物科学与技术研究院	医学部	张华东	zhanghd@xjtu.edu.cn
18	转化医学研究院	医学部	刘成程	liuchengcheng@xjtu.edu.cn
19	管理研究院	管理学院	任博尘	rbc929@xjtu.edu.cn
20	经济金融研究院	经济与金融学院	张 娇	zhangjiaoooo@163.com
21	公共政策与发展研究院	公共政策与管理学院	郁 箐	yuqing1984@xjtu.edu.cn
22	人文与社会科学研究院	人文社会科学学院	刘千瑞	liuqianrui@xjtu.edu.cn
23	法学研究院	法学院	谢毅娟	450062675@qq.com
24	马克思主义与治国理政研究院	马克思主义学院	岳鹏飞	yuepengfei0701@xjtu.edu.cn
25	语言文化及国际交流研究中心	外国语学院	张 颖	angela.zhang@xjtu.edu.cn
26	金禾经济研究中心	金禾经济研究中心	李 芮	lirui123@xjtu.edu.cn
27	新媒体与社会治理研究院	新闻与新媒体学院	孙 雯	sunwen@xjtu.edu.cn
28	实验动物中心	——	刘恩岐	liuenqi@xjtu.edu.cn
29	生物医学中心	——	黄 辰	hchen@xjtu.edu.cn

STARTING FROM iHARBOUR!
从创新港,扬帆起航!

前招三辰，后引凤凰。
朝气蓬勃的创新港敞开
胸怀拥抱世界，
聚天下英才，释磅礴动力，
追复兴之梦！

The vibrant Innovation Harbour embraces the world with open arms, gathers the world's talents, shows the boundless power, and pursues the dream of rejuvenation.